AUSTRALIAN BIRDLIFE

Steve Parish

NATURE kids

EVERY KID'S A NATURE KID

www.steveparish.com.au

WHAT IS A BIRD?

A bird is an animal whose body is covered with feathers. Instead of front limbs, birds have wings. Most birds use their wings to fly.

A bird's legs are covered with scales and its toes end in claws. A bird's jaws are covered by a horny beak. It has no teeth.

The length and shape of a bird's wings, beak and legs give clues to how the bird lives and finds food.

A baby bird develops inside a hard-shelled egg. This egg is kept warm, usually in a nest, until the chick is ready to hatch.

◀ A Sulphur-crested Cockatoo

A Jacky Winter sitting on its nest ▲

FiNE FEATHERS

A bird's feathers keep it warm and dry. Strong wing feathers help the bird to fly. The colour of its feathers helps hide a bird from enemies. Sometimes a female bird is a different colour from the male bird.

Birds preen their feathers with their beaks to keep them neat and clean. Some birds also bathe in water. Each year a bird moults: some of its feathers fall out and new ones grow to replace them.

An Australian Pelican preening ▲

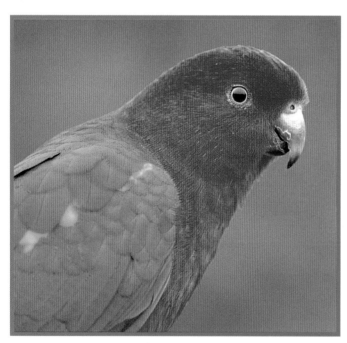

▲ A male Australian King-Parrot

A Plumed Whistling-Duck bathing ▲

A Red-tailed Tropicbird flying ▶

NESTiNG

◀ An Eastern Yellow Robin and chicks

A pair of Black-necked Storks courting ▲

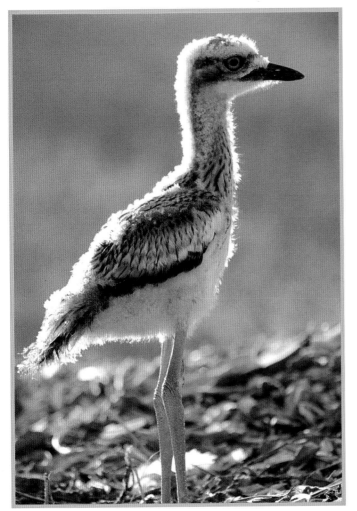

▲ A Bush Stone-curlew chick

When trying to attract a mate, some birds display special feathers. Others sing or dance. Some give each other food, while other birds fly in patterns.

The female bird lays eggs in a nest. The eggs are kept warm until the chicks hatch. The chicks of some birds stay in the nest until they can fly. One or both parents feed the chicks during this time. The chicks of other birds leave the nest soon after hatching and find their own food.

BIG RUNNERS

The Emu and the Southern Cassowary are big, heavy birds. Their wings are small and they cannot fly. They have long, strong legs and can run very fast. They defend themselves by kicking.

Female cassowaries and Emus lay eggs, then leave the males to incubate them (keep them warm). After the chicks hatch, the males look after them until they are ready to survive on their own.

An Emu has long, strong legs. ▶

▲ A male Southern Cassowary keeping his chicks warm

WATERFOWL

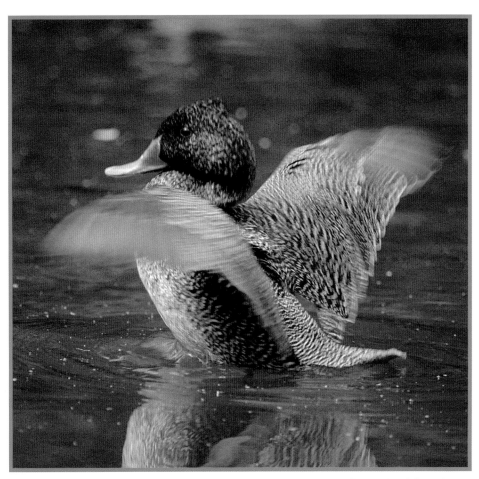

◀ A Black Swan and four cygnets   A Freckled Duck ▲

Ducks, geese and swans are called waterfowl. They have webbed feet and their beaks are covered with soft skin. Most waterfowl are good swimmers.

Female waterfowl line their nests with feathers they pull from their breasts. This keeps the eggs warm when they leave them to find food. The chicks are covered with down (soft feathers). They can swim soon after hatching.

FiSH EATERS

Birds that eat fish must be able to dive and swim well.

Penguins have short, stiff wings like flippers, and webbed feet.

Darters also have webbed feet. They swim under water, then quickly shoot out their long necks and stab fish with their beaks.

▲ A Little Penguin walks with its flippers held out.

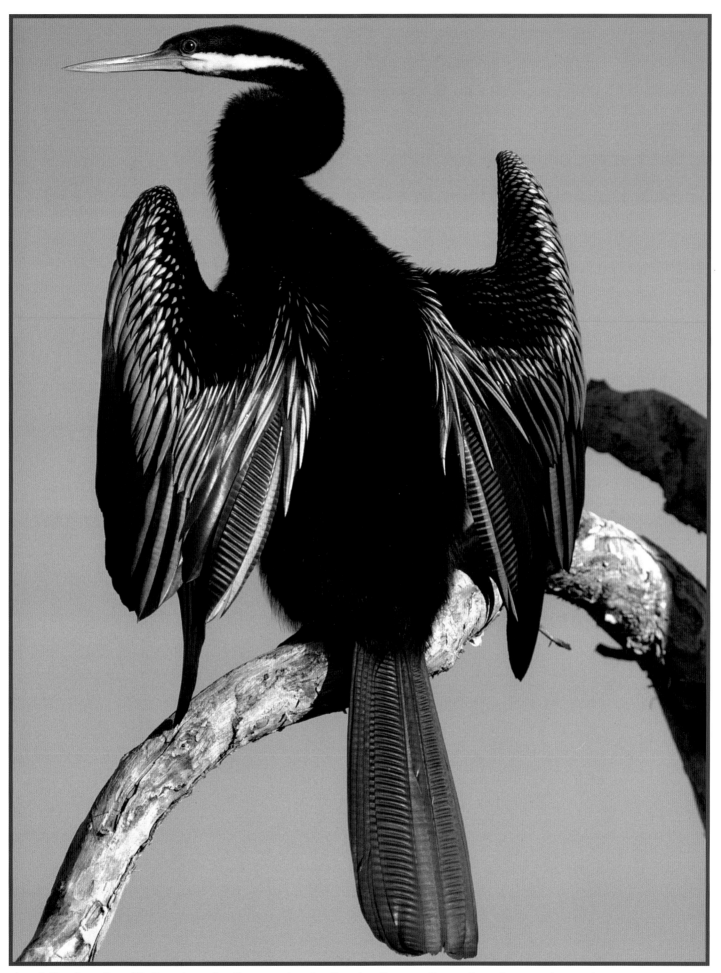

▲ A Darter sits with its wings half-open to dry the feathers after swimming under water.

SEABIRDS

Seabirds can drink salt water. Their bodies use the water, then the left-over salt drips out of their nostrils. Most seabirds have webbed feet and can float or swim. Some can dive.

Gulls find their food on beaches and sometimes eat other seabirds' eggs.

Pelicans eat fish. A flock of pelicans will round up a school of fish. Then they scoop up the fish with their big beaks and swallow them.

▲ A Silver Gull   A flock of Australian Pelicans ▶

FRESHWATER BiRDS

Many birds live on freshwater lakes, swamps and billabongs. Some swim on lakes and ponds in town parks.

Grebes have toes that are wide and flat like paddles. They are good swimmers and divers but can hardly walk on land.

Their floating nests are made of water-weed.

Moorhens can walk as well as swim. They live in groups and build nests amongst reeds. Moorhen chicks swim with their parents during the daytime. At night they sleep on the nest.

◀ An Australasian Grebe and its chicks on a floating nest   A Dusky Moorhen and its chick ▲

PLUMED WATERBIRDS

▲ Yellow-billed Spoonbills at their nest

Egrets, herons and spoonbills have long legs and necks. Herons and egrets wade through water or grass, hunting frogs and fish. Spoonbills swish their beaks through shallow water. They snap up any creature they touch.

In spring, all these birds grow special feathers on their heads and backs. These feathers are called plumes and are shown off by the bird to attract a mate.

▲ An Intermediate Egret on its hunting perch

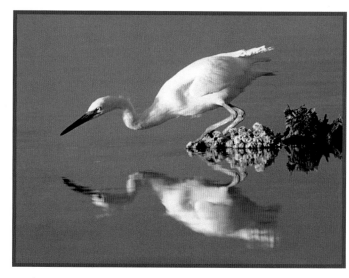

A Reef Egret stabs at a fish. ▲

▲ A Great Egret with two chicks: its long feathers are called plumes.

PLAINS BIRDS

◀ A Masked Lapwing with just-hatched chicks   An Australian Bustard stalks through grassland. ▲

Birds that live on plains have many enemies, such as birds of prey and foxes. Often the feathers of these birds are the same colours as grass or stones. This camouflage colouring helps to hide them from enemies.

The chicks of these birds leave the nest soon after they hatch. When danger is near, they crouch down and stay very still.

▲ A Bush Stone-curlew

BiRDS OF PREY

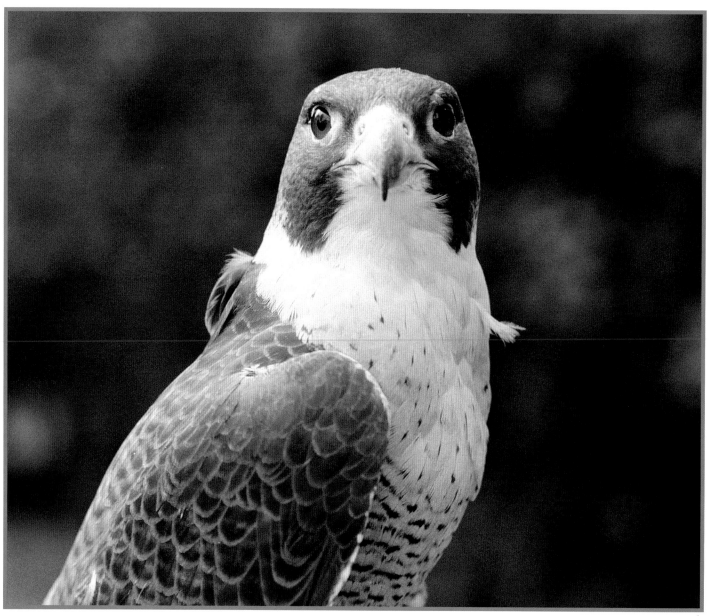

▲ The Peregrine Falcon is one of the fastest flying birds.

Eagles, hawks, falcons and kites feed on other animals. They have strong legs with sharp claws called talons. Their beaks are pointed and curved.

Eagles either catch live prey or feed on dead animals such as road kills. Falcons always catch live prey. They can fly and dive very fast.

A Wedge-tailed Eagle's eyes are much sharper than those of a human. ▶

DOVES & PIGEONS

Doves and pigeons have small heads and plump bodies. Many have bare skin around their eyes. They are fast fliers and often their wings make whirring or whistling noises.

Doves and pigeons that live in the desert eat dry seed, so they need to drink often. They can suck up water without lifting their heads. Then they fly away quickly, because many enemies, such as hawks, hunt near water.

◀ A male Crested Pigeon courting a female

▲ A Spinifex Pigeon drinking at a desert waterhole

PARROTS

▲ A female Eclectus Parrot

A Major Mitchell's Cockatoo ▲

A parrot has a curved beak. Each of its feet has two toes pointing forwards and two pointing backwards. Most parrots are brightly coloured.

Cockatoos are big parrots with crests of feathers on their heads. Lorikeets are small parrots that feed on the nectar from flowers.

▲ Crimson Rosellas bathing

A pair of Rainbow Lorikeets ▶

FR☉GMOUThS

Frogmouths have wide beaks and big mouths. During the day, they pose like dead branch stumps. At night, they hunt insects, frogs and mice. They often hunt near roads. Sometimes they are killed by cars.

A pair of frogmouths builds a stick nest in a tree fork. They take turns to sit on the eggs. After the chicks have left the nest, the family stays together for many weeks.

◀ A Tawny Frogmouth and two chicks at night

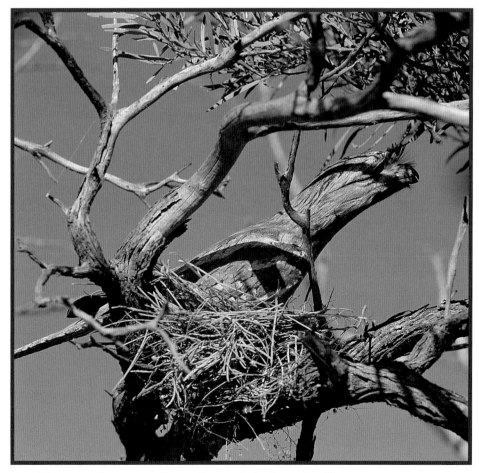

▲ A Tawny Frogmouth on its nest during daytime

OWLS

Owls have narrow, hooked beaks and strong, taloned feet. Their soft feathers make no noise as they hunt small animals at night.

Some sorts of owls have dark eyes and heart-shaped faces. Other sorts of owls have yellow or green eyes. Around each eye is a circle of feathers. All owls see very well in the dark. Their sharp hearing also helps them find prey.

Owls nest in tree hollows, in caves and even in farm sheds.

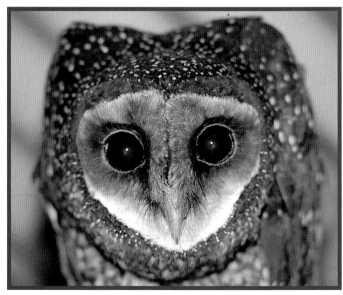

▲ A Barn Owl hunting at night

The rare Sooty Owl lives in rainforest. ▲

▲ A young Barking Owl: it has some adult feathers and some down.

KiNGFiSHERS

◀ A Laughing Kookaburra

A Buff-breasted Paradise-Kingfisher ▲

A kingfisher's beak is long and strong. Some kingfishers catch reptiles, insects, frogs and spiders. Some kingfishers dive for fish.

Kookaburras are very big kingfishers that live in family groups. When chicks hatch, all the family members help feed them. Kookaburras call loudly to tell other birds that they claim an area as their own.

A Forest Kingfisher ▲

LYREBiRDS

▲ A female Superb Lyrebird scratching for food

A male Superb Lyrebird ▶

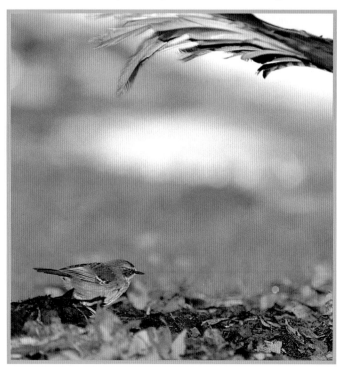

▲ A lyrebird's tail shelters a small, feeding bird.

In spring, a male lyrebird dances in a forest clearing. He spreads his tail and sings loudly. When a female comes along, they mate. The female rears one chick by herself.

Lyrebirds scratch up worms and other creatures from the forest floor. Small birds may follow them, sharing their food.

BUSHLAND BIRDS

Many bushland birds feed in trees, in low bushes or on the ground. Pardalotes are small birds found only in Australia. They eat insects that they catch in the tree tops. In spring, they nest in holes in trees and earth banks.

Fairy-wrens are tiny birds with long tails. A brightly coloured male and a brown female will mate. Other younger birds will help them build a nest that is like a hollow grass ball. All the group helps feed the chicks.

Male Australian robins have bright breasts. Robins feed near the ground. They build nests from bark and cobwebs.

◄ A Striated Pardalote carrying food to its nest, a burrow in an earth bank

▲ A male Red-capped Robin and nest

A male Variegated Wren singing ▲

BOWERBIRDS

A young male bowerbird watches older males build bowers of sticks. When he is old enough, he builds his own bower. Then he gathers treasures, such as berries and flowers, to put in his bower. He sings and dances at the bower to attract a female. She mates with the male, then builds a nest. She lays the eggs, then takes care of them and brings up the chicks all by herself.

◀ A young male Satin Bowerbird singing at a bower

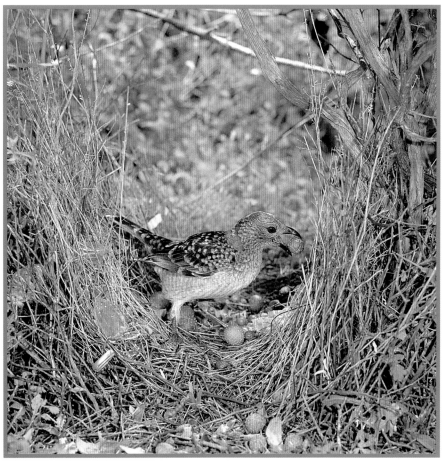

▲ A male Spotted Bowerbird with its treasures in its bower

BLACK & WHITE BIRDS

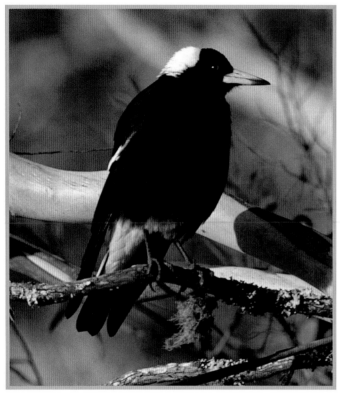

▲ An Australian Magpie

Birds with black and white feathers are called "pied" birds. They often feed and nest near people's houses.

Pied birds, such as magpies, magpie-larks, butcherbirds and currawongs, have loud calls. They call to keep in touch with members of their family. They also call to warn other groups that an area is theirs.

A Pied Butcherbird ▶

▲ A Pied Currawong

A Magpie-lark ▲

HONEYEATERS

Honeyeaters have slender beaks. They poke their beaks into flowers to get the sweet nectar. As they do this, pollen grains stick to their heads. When they visit other flowers, they leave the pollen there. It will help the plant make seeds.

Some honeyeaters live in family groups. A family of Noisy Miners defends its area by shrieking and diving.

▲ A young Blue-faced Honeyeater feeding

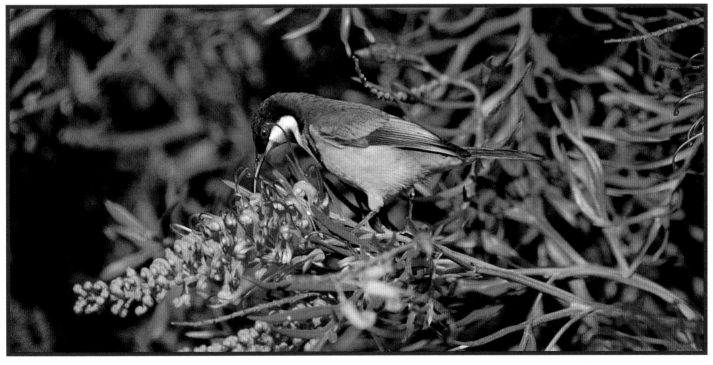

◄ A Noisy Miner feeding on umbrella tree flowers

An Eastern Spinebill on grevillea flowers ▲

FRUiT-EATiNG BiRDS

▲ A female Figbird eating a Carpentaria Palm fruit

▲ This Regent Bowerbird will eat rainforest fruit.

Birds that eat fruit will visit a tree when its fruit is ripe. When all the fruit in an area is finished, the birds move on to another area. The bird swallows the fruit and the hard seed passes out with the droppings. The seed may grow into another tree, some distance away.

▲ White-eyes eat insects and nectar as well as fruit.

GARDENS & BiRDS

Birds will visit a garden to find food such as nectar, seeds or insects. Some birds will drink at a pond or bird bath. Others will bathe in the water. Birds feel safe in a garden that has trees and bushes. They may build nests and bring up chicks there.

▲ A Willy Wagtail

◀ A Crimson Rosella

Red-browed Finches drinking ▲

iNDEX OF BiRDS PiCTURED

First published by Steve Parish Publishing Pty Ltd, 1998
PO Box 1058, Archerfield BC
Queensland 4108, Australia

www.steveparish.com.au

© copyright Steve Parish Publishing Pty Ltd, 1998

ISBN 1 87628 291 6

Photography by Steve Parish with photographic assistance by Darran Leal, SPP, with
p. 8: Stan Breeden
pp. 3, 19, 20, 21 (Bush Stone-curlew), 25, 29, 33 (Buff-breasted Paradise-Kingfisher), 37 (Variegated Wren), 43 (Blue-faced Honeyeater), 47 (Red-browed Finches): Peter Slater
pp. 6, 7 (Bush Stone-curlew), 16, 24–25, 28–29, 31, 34, 36, 37 (Red-capped Robin), 38–39, 39, 42, 44–45: Raoul Slater

Text by Pat Slater

Editing, design and production
Steve Parish Publishing Pty Ltd, Australia

PRINTED IN AUSTRALIA